JUST FORE LAUGHS

America's Favorite Cartoonists Take a Swing at America's Favorite Game

Compiled by Richard Dennison

A PERIGEE BOOK

THE BERKLEY PUBLISHING GROUP
Published by the Penguin Group
Penguin Group (USA) Inc.
375 Hudson Street, New York, New York 10014, USA
Penguin Group (Canada), 10 Alcorn Avenue, Toronto, Ontario M4V 3B2, Canada
(a division of Pearson Penguin Canada Inc.)
Penguin Books Ltd., 80 Strand, London WC2R 0RL, England
Penguin Group Ireland, 25 St. Stephen's Green, Dublin 2, Ireland (a division of Penguin Books Ltd.)
Penguin Group (Australia), 250 Camberwell Road, Camberwell, Victoria 3124, Australia
(a division of Pearson Australia Group Pty. Ltd.)
Penguin Books India Pvt. Ltd., 11 Community Centre, Panchsheel Park, New Delhi—110 017, India
Penguin Group (NZ), Cnr. Airborne and Rosedale Roads, Albany, Auckland 1310, New Zealand
(a division of Pearson New Zealand Ltd.)
Penguin Books (South Africa) (Pty.) Ltd., 24 Sturdee Avenue, Rosebank, Johannesburg 2196,
South Africa

Penguin Books Ltd., Registered Offices: 80 Strand, London WC2R 0RL, England

PRINTING HISTORY
Perigee trade paperback edition / May 2005

PERIGEE is a registered trademark of Penguin Group (USA) Inc.
The "P" design is a trademark belonging to Penguin Group (USA) Inc.

Library of Congress Cataloging-in-Publication Information
Just for laughs : America's cartoonists take a swing at America's favorite game / compiled by Richard
   Dennison.
      p. cm.
    ISBN 0-399-53151-3
    1. Golf—Caricatures and cartoons. 2. American wit and humor, Pictorial. 3. Life—Quotations, maxims,
   etc. I. Dennison, Richard

NC1763.G6J87 2005
741.5'973—dc22
                                                                                    2004058504

PRINTED IN THE UNITED STATES OF AMERICA

10 9 8 7 6 5 4 3 2 1

This book is for my wife Kim. When we were first married I came home after a particularly bad round of golf. I was banging cabinets, yelling at the dog, slamming my clubs around and generally feeling and acting miserable. Kim watched my little tantrum for the umpteenth time and asked me, "If golf always makes you act like this, why do you play the game?" With a face purple with rage, veins popping, in my temple, I answered her. "Because," I screamed, "it's fun."

Honey, it's been more than thirty-seven years and it's still fun.

ACKNOWLEDGEMENTS

Because this book is a compilation of cartoons and quotations it required the assistance, patience, and cooperation of many people. I have tried to list them all below and my sincere apologies to anyone I inadvertently omitted.

Special thanks to Savannah Ashour, Francine Della Catena, James R. Cavett, Gary DaSilva, Cordelia Dyer, Rosemarie Gawelko, Michael Greaves, Naomi Ives, Russell James, Peter Kohlsaat, Boe McBride, Maura Peters, Stephen G. Scholle, Patrick Sheer, Andre Springer, Marianne Sugawara, Mary Suggert, Graig Tenney, and Alice Wilson.

I will be forever grateful to my agent Alice Martell of the Alice Martell Agency and John Duff, publisher, vice president and senior editor, Perigee Books, an imprint of the Penguin Group. Without their enthusiasm and belief in the book, it would not have been published.

And finally, the magnificent cartoonists! These talented guys and gals are true artists. Their creations become like family to us, and they make us laugh on a daily basis, year in and year out. I am in awe of their work and it is with the deepest gratitude that I present a tiny portion of their wonderful creativeness and humor in this book.

REGARDING THE QUOTATIONS…

Some of the quotations in this book fit with the cartoon,
some fit with the category and some, well . . . . you'll figure it out.

ADDICTION

"Mad" is a term we use to describe a man who is
obsessed with one idea and nothing else.

Ugo Betti (1892–1953)
Italian dramatist and poet, *Struggle Till Dawn*

B.C. By Johnny Hart

AFTERLIFE

The only time my prayers are never
answered is on the golf course.

Attributed to Billy Graham (1918–)
U.S. preacher, international evangelist

AGGRAVATION

OSCAR: Everything you do irritates me.
And when you're not here, the things I know you're
gonna do when you come back in irritate me.

Neil Simon (1927–)
U.S. playwright; said to Felix. *The Odd Couple*

BEETLE BAILEY By Mort Walker

ALCOHOL

If all be true that I do think,
There are five reasons we should drink;
Good wine—a friend—or being dry—
Or lest we should be by and by—
Or any other reason why.

Henry Aldrich (1647–1710)
English cleric and scholar, *Reasons for Drinking*

REAL LIFE ADVENTURES By Wise & Aldrich

Shortly after the Scots invented golf,
they invented scotch.

ALIENS

Space—the final frontier . . . These are the voyages of the starship *Enterprise*.
It's five-year mission . . . to boldly go where no man has gone before.

Star Trek
U.S. television series created by Gene Roddenberry

In The Bleachers By Steve Moore

"We saw nothing. Do you understand? Nothing! First of all, no one would believe us. Second, I've got dibs on his golf clubs."

ANGER

The man who gets angry at the right things and
with the right people, and in the right way and at the right time
and for the right length of time, is commended.

Aristotle (384 BC–322 BC)
Greek philosopher, *Nicomachean Ethics*

HAGAR THE HORRIBLE By Dik Browne

ANIMALS

Nothing can be more obvious than that all animals
were created solely and exclusively for the use of man.

Thomas Love Peacock (1785–1866)
Headlong Hall (1816), Ch. 2

BALLARD STREET By Jerry Van Amerongen

ASSISTANCE

People must help one another; it is nature's law.

Jean de La Fontaine (1621–1695)
French writer and poet, *Fables*, *"L'Âne et le Chien"*

In The Bleachers By Steve Moore

"That's the only way Gordon can tee off.
He spent 10 years in the NFL as a
field-goal kicker."

BUDDIES

To like and dislike the same things,
that is indeed true friendship.

Sallust (86?–35? BC)
Roman historian and politician, *Bellum Catilinae*

DENNIS THE MENACE

"THESE GUYS ARE CRONIES."

BUSINESS

Business was his aversion; pleasure was his business.

Maria Edgeworth (1767–1849)
English writer, *The Contrast*, Ch. 1

HI AND LOIS By Brian and Greg Walker

CADDIES

Bind up their wounds—but look the other way.

W. S. Gilbert (1836–1911)
British librettist and playwright, *Princess Ida*

THE WIZARD OF ID By Brant Parker and Johnny Hart

CARTS

They do those little personal things people sometimes
do when they think they are alone in railway carriages; things
like smelling their own armpits.

Jonathan Miller (1934–)
British psychologist, director, and writer, *Beyond the Fringe*

In The Bleachers By Steve Moore

"Try putting it in forward, then quickly shove it into reverse."

CHEATING

If there are obstacles, the shortest line between
two points may be the crooked one.

Bertolt Brecht (1898–1956)
German playwright and poet, *The Life of Galileo*

BEETLE BAILEY By Mort Walker

COURSES

The great landscapist has his own peculiar obsession;
it is a kind of scared horror. His caverns are deep and gloomy;
precipitous rocks threaten the sky . . . man passes through
the domain of demons and gods.

Denis Diderot (1713–1784)
French encyclopedist and philosopher

In The Bleachers By Steve Moore

"This is a tough course."

CURSING

What the dickens!

Thomas Heywood (1574–1641)
English playwright and writer, *Edward IV*

HI AND LOIS By Brian and Greg Walker

DEDICATION

In for a penny, in for a pound.

Anonymous
Proverb

DEMONS

It is no good casting out devils. They belong to us,
we must accept them and be at peace with them.

D. H. Lawrence (1885–1930)
British writer, *Phoenix*, *"The Reality of Peace"*

In The Bleachers By Steve Moore

"I'm serious, Wayne.
I really think that, just this once,
you should go back and replace your divot."

DOCTORS

I used to wonder why people should be so fond of the company of their physician, till I recollected that he is the only person with whom one dares to talk continually of oneself, without interruption, contradiction or censure; I suppose that delightful immunity doubles their fees.

Attributed to Hannah More (1745–1833)
British writer, 1789

BIZARRO By Dan Piraro

DUFFERS

Our dear King James is good and honest, but the
most incompetent man I have ever seen in my life. A child of
seven years would not make such silly mistakes as he does.

Duchess of Orléans (1652–1722)
French sister-in-law to Louis XIV. Referring to James II, who was in exile in France.
Letter to the electress Sophia

THE WIZARD OF ID By Brant Parker and Johnny Hart

DYING

It is a modest creed, and yet
Pleasant if one considers it,
To own that death itself must be,
Like all the rest, a mockery.

Percy Bysshe Shelley (1792–1822)
English poet, "The Sensitive Plant"

THE WIZARD OF ID By Parker and Hart

EMBARRASSMENT

I left the room with silent dignity,
but caught my foot in the mat.

George Grossmith (1874–1912)
British entertainer, singer, and writer, *The Diary of a Nobody*

ENTHUSIASM

There is a melancoholy which accompanies all enthusiasm.

Lord Shaftesbury (1671–1713)
English writer, *Characeristics*, Vol. I, P. *13*

DRABBLE By Kevin Fagan

EQUIPMENT

Apocalypse Now is not about Vietnam, it is Vietnam. We were in the jungle;
there were too many of us; we had access to too much money,
too much equipment; and, little by little, we went insane.

Attributed to Francis Ford Coppola (1939–)
U.S. film director, producer, and screenwriter
Referring to his award-winning movie, *Apocalypse Now*

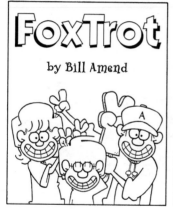

ETIQUETTE

It's all right, Arthur, the white wine came up with the fish.

Attributed to Herman J. Mankiewicz (1897–1953)
U.S. screenwriter and film producer
after vomiting at the table of a fastidious host

PEANUTS By Charles M. Schulz

EXERCISE

Whenever I feel like exercise, I lie down until the feeling passes.

Attributed to Robert M. Hutchins (1899–1977)
U.S. educator

DRABBLE By Kevin Fagan

EXPENSE

But it's easy 'nough to titter w'en de stew is smokin' hot,
But hit's mighty ha'd to giggle w'en dey's nuffin' in de pot.

Paul Laurence Dunbar (1872–1906)
U.S. poet, novelist, and playwright, *The Complete Poems*, "Philosophy"

DRABBLE By Kevin Fagan

FASHION

The Highly Fashionable and the Absolutely Vulgar
are but two faces of the common coin of humanity.

H.G. Wells (1866–1946)
English writer, journalist, and historian, *Select Conversations with an Uncle*

NON SEQUITUR By Wiley

FORE

Golf is a game in which you yell 'fore', shoot six and write down five.

Attributed to Paul Harvey (1918–)
U.S. newscaster and journalist

DRABBLE By Kevin Fagan

FRUSTRATION

Hypochondria torments us not only with causeless irritation with the things of the present; not only with groundless anxiety on the score of future misfortunes entirely of our own manufacture; but also with unmerited self-reproach for our own past actions.

Arthur Schopenhauer (1788–1860)
German philosopher, *Parerga and Paralipomena*

"Did you win?"

FUN

I entertained on a cruising trip that was so much fun
that I had to sink my yacht to make my guests go home.

F. Scott Fitzgerald (1896–1940)
U.S. writer, *"Notebook K"*

beetle
bailey
by mort walker

DID YOU HAVE FUN TODAY SIR?

GOLF IS NOT SUPPOSED TO BE FUN!

WHAT'S FUN ABOUT TRYING TO HIT A LITTLE BALL WITH A LONG STICK 400 YARDS INTO A TINY HOLE?

IS IT FUN TO HIT TREES, LOSE BALLS IN THE WATER OR GO OUT OF BOUNDS?

www.kingfeatures.com

AND, WHEN IT'S ALL OVER, WHAT'S FUN ABOUT HAVING A SCORE LARGER THAN THE NATIONAL DEBT?

6-4

WHY DO YOU PLAY GOLF THEN, SIR?

ON THE OUTSIDE CHANCE THAT SOMEDAY IT MIGHT BE FUN

MORT WALKER

GAMBLING

Man is a gaming animal. He must always be trying
to get the better in something or other.

Charles Lamb (1775–1834)
British essayist, *Essays of Elia*, "Mrs Battle's Opinions on Whist"

BEETLE BAILEY By Mort Walker

HANDICAPS

We hold these truths to be self-evident,
that all men are created equal.

Thomas Jefferson
U.S. President, *Declaration of Independence*

PEANUTS By Charles M. Schulz

HAZARDS

In the jaws of death.

Guillaume du Bartas (1544–1590)
French poet, *Divine Weekes and Workes*, "Second Week, First Day"

In The Bleachers By Steve Moore

HOLE IN ONE

More is owing to what we call chance, that is, philosophically speaking,
to the observation of events arising from unknown causes, than to any
proper design, or pre-conceived theory of the business.

Joseph Priestley (1733–1804)
British theologian and scientist, *Experiments and Observations of Different Types of Air*

IMAGINATION

Hope and imagination are the only consolations
for the disappointments and sorrows of experience.

Italo Calvino (1923–1985)
Cuban-born Italian novelist and short-story writer
Six Memos for the Next Millennium, "Exactitude" (*Patrick Creagh [tr.]*)

Pluggers

The plugger golfer thinks of himself as as a 90's kind of guy, even though he rarely breaks 100.

IMPROVEMENT

What we call progress is the exchange of one
nuisance for another nuisance.

Havelock Ellis (1859–1939)
British psychologist, *Impressions and Comments*

In The Bleachers By Steve Moore

"That's it! I did it! I finally figured out how to hit the perfect golf shot every single time!!"

INSTRUCTION

That is what learning is. You suddenly understand something you've understood all your life, but in a new way.

Doris Lessing (1919–)
British novelist and short-story writer, *The Four-Gated City*

CLOSE TO HOME By John McPherson

Told by his golf instructor to "be the ball,"
Ron visualizes his upcoming putt.

INSULTS

And you, madam, are ugly.
But I shall be sober in the morning.

Attributed to Winston Churchill (1874–1965)
British prime minister and writer
Replying to the member of Parliament Bessie Braddock, who told him he was drunk.

BLONDIE By Dean Young and Denis Lebrun

KIBITZERS

A great master of gibes and flouts and jeers.

Benjamin Disraeli (1804–1881)
British prime minister and writer
Referring to Lord Salisbury, *Hansard, Speech in the British Parliament*

SHOE By Jeff MacNelly

LIES

Ask no questions and hear no lies.

Anonymous

Proverb

HAGAR THE HORRIBLE By Dik Browne

FAREWELL, HELGA! I SAIL AWAY ON THE TIDE TO INVADE **SCOTLAND!**

WHERE ARE YOUR **GOLF** CLUBS?

DOES IT **LOOK** LIKE I'M TAKING MY GOLF CLUBS?

NO...

SCOTLAND HAS GREAT COURSES, BUT THIS IS A **BUSINESS** TRIP

SO, WHERE **ARE** YOUR CLUBS?

ON THE **BOAT**

CHRIS BROWNE 9-20

LOST BALLS

I shot an arrow into the air,
It fell to earth, I knew not where.

Henry Wadsworth Longfellow (1807–1882)
U.S. poet, "The Arrow and the Song"

1-23

© Jim Unger/dist. by United Media, 1998

**"Of course you never lose *your* ball …
you never hit it more than a few feet."**

LUCK

The hardest shot in golf is the 90-yard wedge,
where the ball has to be played off a tree,
bounce back into a bunker, hit a stone, bounce onto the green,
roll to the cup, hit the pin and drop in the hole.
That shot is so tough I've only made it once.

Attributed to Zeppo Marx (1901–1979)
U.S. actor and comedian

HAGAR THE HORRIBLE By Dik Browne

MARSHALS

Bad boys, bad boys, what ya gonna do?
What ya gonna do when they come for you?

Opening theme song lyrics of 20th Century Fox TV show, *Cops*
Performed by Inner Circle, written by Ian Lewis

DRABBLE By Kevin Fagan

MEDIA

Television? No good will come of this device.
The word is half Greek and half Latin.

Attributed to C. P. Scott (1846–1932)
British journalist

NOVICES

Some people will never learn anything, for this
reason, because they understand everything too soon.

Alexander Pope (1688–1744)
English essayist, *Thoughts on Various Subjects*

O.B.

Punishment is not for revenge,
but to lessen crime and reform the criminal.

Elizabeth Fry (1780–1845)
British prison reformer

HAVE YOU EVER NOTICED HOW, AT THIS TIME OF YEAR, THE RAYS OF THE SUN REFLECT OFF THE SHINY WHITE PAINT ON THE "OUT OF BOUNDS" STAKES?

OFFICE

For many wage earners work is perceived as a
form of punishment which is the price to be paid
for various kinds of satisfactions away from the job.

Douglas McFregor (1906–1964)
U.S. management theorist, *The Human Side of Enterprise*

REAL LIFE ADVENTURES By Wise and Aldrich

PARENTING

The gods
Visit the sins of the fathers upon the children.

Euripides (480?–406 BC)
Greek playwright, *Phrixus*

HAGAR THE HORRIBLE By Dik Browne

PHILOSOPHY

I have a simple philosophy. Fill what's empty.
Empty what's full. And scratch where it itches.

Alice Lee Longworth (1884–1980)
U.S. society figure

BEETLE BAILEY By Mort Walker

PLAYING THROUGH

It does no harm to throw the occasional man overboard,
but it does not do much good if you are steering full speed ahead for the rocks.

Ian Gilmour (1926–)
British politician, lobbyist, and writer
Said after being fired as deputy foreign secretary, *Time* magazine

OVER THE HEDGE By Michael Fry and T. Lewis

comics.com

WHEN PLAYING SLOWLY IT'S ALWAYS POLITE TO LET FASTER PARTIES ...

BEEP!
BEEP!

...PLAY THROUGH.

7-28

POLITICALLY INCORRECT

'There's been an accident,' they said,
'Your servant's cut in half; he's dead!'
'Indeed!' said Mr. Jones, 'and please
send me the half that's got my keys.'

Harry Graham (1874–1936)
British writer, poet, and dramatist, *Ruthless Rhymes for Heartless Homes*; 'Mr.Jones'

GET FUZZY. By Darby Conley

POWER

A sense of power is the most intoxicating

stimulant a mortal can enjoy . . .

Ellen Swallow Richards (1842–1911)

U.S. chemist and applied researcher, *The Life of Ellen H. Richards (Caroline L. Hunt)*

BALLARD STREET By Jerry Van Amerongen

PRACTICE

In all things, success depends upon previous preparation,
and without such preparation there is sure to be failure.

Confucius (551–479 BC)
Chinese philosopher analects

MOTHER GOOSE AND GRIMM By Mike Peters

PROS

I've always made a total effort, even when the odds seemed entirely against me.
I never quit trying; I never felt that I didn't have a chance to win.

Arnold Palmer (1929–)
U.S. professional golfer

In The Bleachers By Steve Moore

Arnold Palmer as a kid

PUTTING

When you suffer an attack of nerves you're being attacked by the nervous system.
What chance has a man got against a system?

Russell Hoban (1925–)
U.S.-born British novelist, children's writer, and illustrator
The Lion of Boaz-Jachin and Jachin-Boaz

In The Bleachers By Steve Moore

"It'll probably break toward the water."

QUITTING

Once I moved like the wind.
Now I surrender to you, and that is all.

Geronimo (1829–1909)
Native American Chiricahua Apache leader
Remark to U.S. troops upon his submission
He escaped from military custody the next day

DRABBLE® By FAGAN

RIDICULE

Look for the ridiculous in everything and you will find it.

Jules Renard (1864–1910)
French writer, *Journal*

CRANKSHAFT By Tom Batiuk and Chuck Ayers

ROUGH

Then welcome each rebuff
That turns earth's smoothness rough,
Each sting that bids nor sit nor stand, but go!
Be our joys three-parts pain!
Strive, and hold cheap the strain;
Learn, nor account the pang; dare, never grudge the throe!

Robert Browning (1812–1889)
British poet, *Dramatis Personae*, "Rabbi Ben Ezra"

JEFF MacNELLEY'S SHOE BY Chris Cassatt and Gary Brookins

RULES

I see but one rule: to be clear. If I am not clear, all my world crumbles to nothing.

Henri Beyle Stendhal (1783–1842)
Reply to Balzac (October 30, 1840)

OVER THE HEDGE By Michael Fry and T. Lewis

SAND

Mock on, Mock on, Voltaire, Rousseau:
Mock on, Mock on: 'tis all in vain!
You throw the sand against the wind,
And the wind blows it back again.

William Blake (1757–1827)
British poet, painter, engraver, and mystic, *Manuscript Notebooks*

IN THE BLEACHERS By Steve Moore

"It's no use! Save yourselves!
Go on to the next hole!"

SCORING

One should always generalize.

Karl Gustav Jakob Jacobi (1804–1851)
German mathematician

GET FUZZY By Darby Conley

SENIORS

Let us take care that age does not make
more wrinkles on our spirit than on our face.

Michel de Montaigne (1533–1592)

French essayist

beetle bailey By Mort Walker

SHAME

JESSICA: What! Must I hold a candle to my shames?

William Shakespeare (1564–1616)
English poet and playwright, *The Merchant of Venice Act 2, Scene 6*

SLICE

No matter how thin you slice it, it's still baloney.

Al Smith (1873–1944)
U.S. politician, *Campaign Speeches, Speech*

CLOSE TO HOME By John McPherson

5-19

"Worst slice I ever saw!"

SPONSOR

All to have promotion—That is their whole devotion!

John Skelton (1460?–1529)
English poet and satirist, *Collyn Clout*, "The Prelates"

CITIZEN DOG By Mark O'Hare

SPOUSES

Men don't understand anything about women and women understand nothing about men. And it's better that way.

Attributed to Vittorio Gassman (1922–2000)

Italian actor

beetle bailey By Mort Walker

TIGER

Tyger! Tyger! burning bright
In the forests of the night,
What immortal hand or eye
Could frame thy fearful symmetry?

William Blake (1757–1827)
British poet, painter, engraver, and mystic, *Songs of Experience*, "The Tyger"

CITIZEN DOG By Mark O'Hare

SHOULD I CHIP FROM HERE?

IT'S UP TO YOU, SIR.

WOULD TIGER WOODS CHIP WITH A WOOD FROM HERE?

I DON'T KNOW, SIR.

HOW MUCH WOOD WOULD A TIGER WOODS CHIP IF A TIGER WOODS WOULD CHIP WOOD ?!?

AHHH-HA-A-HA-HA HA HA HA HA HA HA HA

GOLF HUMOR.

VERY FUNNY, SIR.

TIPS

The purpose of human life is to serve and
to show compassion and the will to help others.

Albert Schweitzer (1875–1965)
German theologian, philosopher, physician, and musicologist

DRABBLE By Kevin Fagan

TOURNAMENTS

A beautiful painting is only a copy of nature;
a beautiful ballet is nature herself, enhanced by all the charms of art . . .
we must not merely practice steps; we must study the passions!

Jean Georges Noverre (1727–1810)
French dancer, choreographer, and ballet master

IN THE Bleachers By Steve Moore

TRAINING AIDS

Men love to wonder, and that is the seed of our science,
And such is the mechanical determination of our age, and so recent are our
best contrivances, that use has not dulled our joy and pride in them.
These arts open great gates of a future, promising to make the world plastic and to
lift human life out of its beggary to a godlike ease and power.

Ralph Waldo Emerson (1803–1882)
U.S. poet and essayist, *Society and Solitude,* "Works and Days"

9-17

"It's called 'Spring-A-Swing.' Yesterday he sliced
a drive that went in one side of a Winnebago
and out the other."

TRIBUTE

Render therefore to all their dues;
tribute to whom tribute is due;
custom to whom custom;
fear to whom fear;
honour to whom honour.

King James Bible
Romans, 13:7

GARFIELD®

TROUBLE

His wigs were a constant source of trouble, for they were not only
dirty and unkempt, but generally burnt away in front, for, being very nearsighted,
he often put his head into the candle when poring over his books.

Charlotte Papendiek (1765–1839)
English diarist referring to Samuel Johnson

Ballard Street By Jerry Van Amerongen

PERRY HAS HIS PROBLEMS OVER ON TWELVE

WAGGLE

The human body is a machine which winds its own springs:
the living image of perpetual movement.

Julien Offroy de La Mettrie (1709–1751)
French philosopher and physician, *The Man-Machine*

CRANKSHAFT By Tom Batiuk and Chuck Ayers

WATER

From the waterfall he named her,
Minnehaha, Laughing Water.

Henry Wadsworth Longfellow (1807–1882)
U.S. poet *The Song of Hiawatha*, "Hiawatha and Mudjekeewis"

JEFF MacNELLY'S SHOE By Chris Cassatt and Gary Brookins

WEATHER

DUKE SENIOR: Hath not old custom made this life more sweet
Than that of painted pomp? Are not these woods
More free from peril than the envious court?
Here feel we but the penalty of Adam,
The seasons' difference; as, the icy fang
And churlish chiding of the winter's wind,
Which, when it bites and blows upon my body,
Even till I shrink with cold, I smile and say,
"This is no flattery."

William Shakespeare (1564–1616)
English poet and playwright, *As You Like It*, Act 2, Scene 1

PICKLES By Brian Crane

WILDLIFE

Learn from the beasts the physic of the field.

Alexander Pope (1688–1744)
English poet, *An Essay on Man*

IN THE BLEACHERS By Steve Moore

"Help me, Meester Golfer!
Help me, help me, help me!!"

PERMISSIONS / CREDITS / COPYRIGHTS